NEGOTIATIONS WITH THE CHILL WIND

NEGOTIATIONS WITH THE CHILL WIND

John Hughes

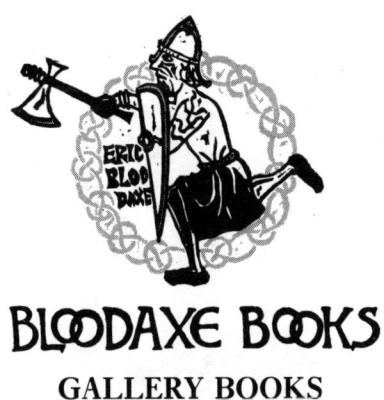

BLOODAXE BOOKS
GALLERY BOOKS

Copyright © John Hughes 1991

ISBN: 1 85224 174 8

First published 1991 by
Bloodaxe Books Ltd,
P.O. Box 1SN,
Newcastle upon Tyne NE99 1SN.

Published simultaneously in Ireland
by The Gallery Press.

Bloodaxe Books Ltd acknowledges
the financial assistance of Northern Arts.

LEGAL NOTICE
All rights reserved. No part of this book may be
reproduced, stored in a retrieval system, or
transmitted in any form, or by any means, electronic,
mechanical, photocopying, recording or otherwise,
without prior written permission from The Gallery Press,
Loughcrew, Oldcastle, Co. Meath, Ireland.

ACKNOWLEDGEMENTS
Acknowledgements are due to the editors of the following
publications in which some of these poems first appeared:
*Ambit, Krino, The London Review of Books, The New Younger
Irish Poets* (Blackstaff Press, 1991), *The Poetry Book Society
Anthology* (PBS/Hutchinson, 1990), *Quarry* (Canada) and
The Times Literary Supplement.

DESIGN & PRODUCTION
Book design & editing: Peter Fallon, The Gallery Press.
Cover design: Bloodaxe Books.
Cover reproduction: V & H Reprographics, Newcastle upon Tyne.
Cover printing: Index Print, Newcastle upon Tyne.

Printed in Great Britain by
Bell & Bain Limited, Glasgow, Scotland.

Contents

Façades *page* 9
The Method 10
Sirius 11
A Little Death Under Charles's Wain 12
Prairie-Girl 13
Endgame 14
Relativity Avenue 14
Nostalgia 15
Pyewackett 16
The Resurrection 17
Star-Bride 18
The Gates of Ivory 19
The Rafters 20
Where the Light Begins 21
Bedtime Story 21
The Story-Teller 22
Natural Disasters 23
The Forecast 24
Lightning Struck Again 25
Journey Aboard the *Argo Navis* 26
Alchemy: A Tale 28
Priest 28
Babylon Tide 28
The Viceroy's Oak 29
Antimony Sulfide 30
The Rat's Ambition 31
Fata Morgana: Annaghmakerrig 32
Chimerical Voyage 32
The Big House on the Hill 33
The Astronomer 34
Ghost of the Brain 35
Where She Was 36
The Veteran 37
The Chambermaid 38
Fairytale Doctors 38

Mexico   39
Two Plus One   40
Twig   41
Stare   41
Black Friday   42
Last Respects   43
Nagasaki   44
New Star   45
Sukkoth: The Ninth Day   45
Shadows   46
The Chill Wind   47
Elijah's Wagon   48
The Arrow   49
The Church   50
Awe   50
Talk of the Devil   51
The Jackdaw   52
The Royal Asylum   53
Death of a Fabulist   54
Treachery   55
Eve   56
Fontaine the Stoat and Valentine the Hare   57
The Left Hand of Oblivion   58
Savage   59
The Tiger's Tail   60
In Time of Plague   61
Three Days of the Cho War   61
On the Block   62
Closing the Book   63

for Mary

'Beauty is dangerous in narrow times, a knife in the slender neck of the rational man, and only those who live between the layers of these strange days can know its name.'

– Don De Lillo

Façades

We drove for hours to reach Castleward,
The big house with two façades:
The south-east front Classical,
The north-east front pure Gothic.

I informed her this was the result
Of a disagreement between
Lord Bangor and his wife, Lady Anne —
His penchant Classical, hers Gothic.

Hunkered under a giant oak,
After circling the house three times,
She told me there was someone else.

I didn't plead and she didn't explain.
I drove her home at speed
A different road from the one we came.

The Method

My love explains to a class of one
The fourfold methods of interpreting the Pentateuch:
Literal, allegorical, tropological, anagogic.
I sit at the rear of the lecture-theatre
Day-dreaming about hanging Munch's
Starry Night above our bed.

And then I am travelling under those same stars,
From Ballyhornan, through Alphaville,
To the offices of *La Croix*,
Where a reporter asks the question,
'Are you?'
        There is a silence
That will not be broken until I decide
Which of four ways I should or shouldn't answer him.
And then it will be too late.

Sirius

When the snowstorm had abated
We lay flat on our backs
On the roof of the Planetarium
And she pointed out Sirius,

Claiming her grandfather Palomar
Had devoted the last months
Of his forty-nine years
To proving that that star

Was the thirty-second path of secret wisdom
As seen in a vision by a prophet
Whose name had been deleted
From the Bible since 1568.

How long were we lying there?
As long as takes a snowflake
To melt on the lens of a telescope
Pointed at the noonday sun.

A Little Death Under Charles's Wain

A dog howled at the Starry Plough.
'Listen to the music of erudition!
It sings to the Emperor Charlemagne,'
She shouted as we wended our way
Through Charles University.

'There's so much you need to know,'
She said when we reached her apartment
In the shadow of Hradcany Castle.

But there was little mystery:
She was another stranger who sweated blood
Until her face turned blue,
And who with her last breath
Called me king of kings.

Prairie-Girl

You remember playing hide-and-seek
on the edge of the prairie —

how you were discovered at sunset
by a neighbour and his coydog —

how walking home your shadow was so huge
it crossed the entire state.

Your mother locked you in your room
for five days and four nights:

you were weightless and lay under
a heavy quilt the whole time

for fear of floating away
into that region of still-life

where there is no shelter
for a thousand miles,

and where an obliterating wind blows
for the lifetime of a watching and waiting girl.

Endgame

While I washed the bloodstained bedclothes
She sketched a map of the constellation Gemini.
When it was finished she pinned it above
The photograph of Bobby Fischer and Boris Spassky
Playing their last game in Reykjavik.
'Bobby and Boris, Castor and Pollux,'
She said as I switched off the light
On the last day of our life together.

Relativity Avenue

Bergson the lighthouseman
and Minkowski the ballerina
are standing on the corner of Relativity Avenue
engrossed in a discussion concerning the cosmology
that suggests an oscillating universe —
explosion, expansion, contraction,
explosion et cetera, ad infinitum —
when a double-parked car-bomb goes off
and blows them to uncountable finite shreds.

I walk along what remains of Relativity Avenue,
denouncing the word *cosmology*
as fatal to the world with method in it —
the world we make up as we go along.

Nostalgia

After Fitz had beaten her within an inch of her life
He rambled about the virtues of absolute fidelity.
When she confessed to having slept with his brother
He walked to Erenagh to shout her name to the ghosts
Of White Frank O'Hare and Edgar Allan Doyle.

They took it upon themselves to remind him
She was the only woman he'd ever loved,
Or was ever likely to love.
'Goodbye and good luck,' they shouted after him
As he ran home to embrace and forgive her.

That night he dreamt she was dying
And there was nothing he could do
But wipe the sweat from her brow.
He woke to find her wake in progress.
A hundred hours later he scrawled in his diary:

Already I feel such nostalgia for her —
The angel who danced on the head of the needle
I threaded through my mother's eye.

Pyewackett

He claimed he could transmute all metals into gold;
that he could make himself invisible,
cure all diseases, and administer an elixir
against old age and the common cold.

He was accused of being an onomancer,
a sternomancer, a gastromancer,
an omphalomancer, an onchyomancer,
and an agent of the police.

You slept with him for three nights.
On the first night he bruised your breasts.
On the second night he scratched your belly.
On the third night he called out my name.

The Resurrection

After a thousand night-time miles
The train pulls into a siding
And the driver climbs out of his cab,
Crosses the tracks and sits down
On the stump of a catalpa tree:
He is enveloped in a whitish dazzle of fog.

෴

It is a dream I have on journeys
To places you will not travel to
Because they remind you of home —
A youngish man sitting on top of you
Until you submitted and played dead
For him to bring you back to life.

Star-Bride

At first light the angel asked Cliona if she was one of seven sisters. She wouldn't answer. With that the angel changed into a bull. He charged and impaled her on his ten horns. She watched her entrails spilling out.

She woke up sprawled out on Paris Braes; and for an instant she wanted to ask if there was anything about the dark she should be afraid of.

I was staring up at the Pleiades when she kissed me on the back of my neck. I called her my star-bride.

The Gates of Ivory

That evening the temperature fell
To something like thirteen below.
Your taxi skidded on black ice
En route to Rue de la Vielle Lanterne

And your sister's *cri de coeur*:
'Where is my promised secret life?
The one in which I am the Armagh Angel
Who debates with Albert Einstein

Whether the geometry of cosmic space
Is Euclidean or non-Euclidean;
The one in which I am Arcturus
Standing guard at the Gates of Ivory,

Quizzing a syphilitic astronomer
About the woman he knew,
What he meant when he talked about love
Dismantling the infinite darkness.'

The Rafters

On the eve of his thirteenth birthday
Fitz stood at Doyle's Corner
Watching a team of shooting stars
Plough across the August sky.

He gritted his teeth and wished
That sky would miraculously peel back
To reveal the huge oak rafters
He had dreamt held it in place.

It was the last wish of his childhood.

The next day he was given a telescope.

That night he could see nothing for clouds.

Where the Light Begins

Some nights I can still remember
How I tracked down by scent alone
The last she-wolf in Ireland
To the last forest. For nine years

We talked about the future behind us.
And when her fangs at last began to show
I fired into her heart a silver bullet,
And headed west to where the light begins.

Bedtime Story

He peers through the telescope
at his neighbour's gold tooth.
It's so cold she undresses in bed.

He trains the telescope
on four horsemen galloping across
a river red with the blood
of grey wolves and only children.

She asks what's keeping him up,
and he replies: 'One, two, three, four.'

The Story-Teller

In a weather-stripped house behind tall gates
we danced in circles and triangles
to scratched 78s of Bessie Smith,
before going for a swim in the canal —
closed a century before by a Lord Lieutenant
with a morbid fear of barges.

On our second dive we discovered
an Anglepoise, an Armalite,
and an execrable sonnet of uncertain age —
whose discovery together, according to her,
was an omen I wouldn't return to the house.
And because I am the story-teller
it was she, not I, who dived a third time
and never came up again.

Natural Disasters

One fine morning an old Hasid
told me he'd been waiting years
for a tornado to blow in off the prairie
and raze the town to the ground.

We stared at a speck on the horizon
and agreed it was the Paschal Lamb.

That speck was the tornado
which killed my first love.

Staring into her waterlogged grave
the old man said he'd begun the long wait
for the local river to burst its banks,
when an incestuous brother and sister
are drowned by their parents
a thousand miles upstream.

The Forecast

We listen to the late weather-bulletin.
The forecast is for severe storms,
resulting in spires and chimneys
being blown down on top of those citizens
who venture out of doors
to post letters to relations
serving sentences in Her Majesty's Prisons.

These letters explain why there is a revival
of the species of dance known as the minuet —
which the citizens describe
as the kingpin of social dances —
and wax lyrical about great Lords and Ladies
dancing with dainty little steps and glides,
to the right and to the left,
forward and backward, in quarter turns,
approaching and retreating hand in hand,
searching and evading, now side by side,
now facing, now gliding past one another.

These letters fail to mention the mob of peasants
tearing down the palace-gates,
streaming into the courtyard,
jumping through the windows of the ballroom,
and into a three-line footnote
of an obscure contemporary chronicle
no one had read for a hundred years —
no one until an elderly history professor
re-discovered it in the university coal-cellar,
as he sheltered from the civil war
raging above his head.

As we climb the stairs to bed you say,
'The weather forecast never gets it right.
Don't you agree?' I'm afraid I do.

Lightning Struck Again

October 1986. Wexford. That rainswept Thursday
a Kerry Blue barked at us
as we stood beneath a 200-year-old oak
which had been struck by lightning
minutes before we happened by.
I asked you not to leave me. But you did.
I stood there pondering the words,
Organic, Relation, Art, Life,
till lightning struck and struck again.

Journey Aboard the Argo Navis

Tropical dark. She rolled onto her belly.
I could hear Claudius Ptolemaeus describe
To a disbelieving Geraldus Mercator
The creation of the universe in terms
Of salt, sulfur, and mercury.
She poked me in the ribs and asked,
'How long before we cross the damned equator?'
I climbed onto deck and waited for a sign.

For ten hours thirty minutes I stared at the ocean,
Till I heard a lion roar and saw the meteor shower
Leonid
Cascading across the November sky.
When I told her we had crossed the celestial equator
She said in an hysterical tone,
'Always do as you have done tonight
And dip not into the waters of the deep
For there are more things in heaven than on earth'.

And so I wiped her brow and waited for our ship
To sail over the edge of the world
Into the gaping jaws of the Great Bear.

Alchemy: A Tale

Un mystère d'amour dans le métal repose – GÉRARD DE NERVAL

A certain man flew from Chicago to his native Golden Vale
To resurrect a recurring dream from his childhood.
The dream: A Frenchman called Lavoisier
Being cooked in a bath till he revealed
The whereabouts of the long-lost philosopher's stone —
The stone which is not a stone.

But his dream brought him to the attention
Of the Angel of Desolation Island
Who took him to Max Brod's city of evil
To stand trial for an unspecified mortal sin
Before Cardinals, Silver, Iron, Tin, and Lead.
They called his sentence of death *Transmutation*,
Washed their hands of him in sulfur water,
Processed into Wenceslaus Square,
And corroded into the nothingness of Mercurial Lore
Screaming, 'One nature rejoices in another nature,
One nature masters another nature'.

A certain man was burnt to death on Desolation Island
By an unflickering, non-luminous tongue of fire.

Priest

He sits on the holiest of holy mountains,
holding a glass of his mother's blood
between his thumb and forefinger,
and talks to a stoat-faced pooka
about the foul-mouthed misogynist
he was once and will be again
when the mountain erodes to a pebble
lodged beneath his swollen tongue.

Babylon Tide

Mrs Babylon spoke in a soft voice
about youthful happiness and uncertain love.
'Where do I begin and end?'
She asked as we reached the water's edge
and the last thirty seconds of summertime.

She went out with the tide
to be washed up further down the coast
with the Black Death, Leviathan,
a splinter of the One True Cross,
the heads of Ursa Major and Ursa Minor.

The Viceroy's Oak

A piebald mare stands beneath the oak
planted by order of the Viceroy of Ireland
in the spring of 1848.

One year ago I sat in its shade
telling my sister how it is
that a name has a place,
and not the other way round.
She called me an ignoramus.

As I approach the horse it canters away
in the direction of the brae
which is really a sleeping giant's back.

Tonight I will lie in a darkened room
at the top of a condemned house
and count the rings of a tree
I have climbed to be terrified
of something more than heights.

Antimony Sulfide

The grey wolf devours the king
on the banks of the shimmering Shimna,
after which it is burned on a pyre —
consuming the wolf and restoring the king
to a life dedicated to proving the feasibility
of alchemical transmutation.

I met this king in Mar del Plata.
We had dinner in the casino.
He had a voracious appetite
for goose and goose eggs.

Our topics of conversation: sulfide scums,
allegorical recipes for refining gold,
the number of counterfeiters
Sir Isaac Newton sent to the gallows
in his job as warden of the Royal Mint,
and, finally, who would pay for dinner.

He paid when I began to howl
for the rest of the pack.

The Rat's Ambition

A rat clambers over my face.
I grab it by the tail,
rub spittle along its back,
and christen it Columbus.

I take the rat along with me
when I travel into the city
to purchase a 1506 map of Hispaniola
and a Genoese *mappemonde* circa 1300.

But in Jerusalem Street the rat scurries
under the wheels of an army Saracen
in search of the tread-mill
that will be its path back
to the fetid hole of the caravel
anchored in the Serpent's Mouth.

It is the rat's ambition to swim ashore
and gnaw through the rib-cage
of the last European sailor
to believe the earth was flat.

It will be an unfulfilled ambition:
a strong current will carry the rat
along the sweet-smelling sewer
discharging the effluent of a New World
into my buttonhole of a mouth.

Fata Morgana: Annaghmakerrig

Where the spruce became pine
She appeared and disappeared in a minute.
Of course she said something apocalyptic;
And yes I vowed to commit to memory
The other, safer way through the forest
In the few hours left to me
That side of the tortuous border.

Chimerical Voyage

The captain's first order of the day
was for the cabin-boy to jump ship
when he issued his second order —
to weigh anchor in weird shadows
for the chimerical continent.

The captain lay in his pus-stained bunk,
leaving the crew to their own devices.
They sailed in ever-decreasing circles
and mutinied on the seventh day.

They tied the captain to the helm
and huddled around him,
as once again he sailed toward
that beach of bleached bones
at the heart of a shipwreck.

The Big House on the Hill

Who lived in the big house on the hill?
The woman who had written a book
about the influence of the Julian calendar
on Volume One of *Tristram Shandy*.

Was it chance or choice which brought her
to the big house on the hill?
A chance meeting with my Uncle Tobias
outside the Cock and Bull Inn.

Each morning she'd light the only fire in the house —
that is until I set the whole place ablaze
with ninety-nine parts carelessness
to one part malice aforethought.

The Astronomer

I had had little sleep since being told,
By the astronomer I'd married the previous week,
Of the postulate that cosmic space curves —
That we inhabit a non-Euclidean universe.
Before I got a chance to question her on this
She flew out on the red-eye to Leipzig,
To attend a year-long conference entitled,
'James Joyce: A Cosmology of the Vanities'.

The next occasion on which we were to meet
Was a decade later. She appeared naked,
With the Great Bear on a long leash,
At the gates of my crumbling villa
On the western edge of Ptolemy's known world.
When I told her to torment some other recluse
She closed her eyes and bared her yellow teeth.
I opened the gates and fell asleep on my feet.

Then I understood this was a nightmare,
And that I was compelled by arbitrary laws
To ask if she would be my child-bride.
She said this would be an impossibility
As her father was dying of leukemia
And had implored her to sleep with him
And confess to the Angel of White Corpuscles
Their unnatural acts, their secret fulfilment.

Woken by the crackle of a distant firefight
I discovered her sprawled out beside me.
'Where is it you come from?' I asked.
She turned her face to the wall and whispered,
'If you must know, I'm from here —
From this flea-ridden bed of yours'.
With that she burst into tears
And wet the bed for the umpteenth time.

'What is it in you such melodramatics conceal?
Are you afraid that you're the lamb facing the wolf,
The ritual slaughter, the sacrificial fire?'
I ask as my vision blurred and my mouth dried up
And I began to die that death again
In the arms of a complete stranger
Who smells of pine-needles, woodsmoke,
Formaldehyde, me.

Ghost of the Brain

The important thing is what we remember
when such and such a woman leaves the room
as the sun sets just before 4 o'clock
on a frosty Sunday in November:
the faint wrinkles around her eyes,
the way she says Pandora's Box,
how she holds her breath after singing a song
about a woman who pities a man
who wants the said woman to tell him
he will never be a ghost of her brain.

Where She Was

She telephoned from Place de l'Étoile
to say she would be home late
as her bus had run over and killed
the milliner who'd stolen from the Louvre
Delacroix's *The Taking of Constantinople
by the Crusaders on April 12, 1204.*

When I asked if the painting had been recovered
she replied that that was the business of no one
but her, the bus-driver, and the *pied noir*
who ran out of the gawping crowd
and bundled the corpse into a taxi.

Whoever was with her whispered
to hurry up before it was too late.

When she slammed the phone down
I was happy I knew where she was
on the night she was supposed
to tell me how she feels compelled
to talk to kepis, electrodes,
hypodermics, and bus-drivers,
about the 100 inch telescope
hastening the end of the world.

The Veteran

In my history of the millenium's end
I described at great length
how the general led a thousand men
across ten rivers and a mountain-range,
fought one battle, razed four towns,
and carried out seventeen massacres
of women, invalids, and children —
how on the long march home
the general died of a burst appendix,
seven hundred soldiers of dysentry,
two hundred of sleeping-sickness,
and ninety-nine of typhoid.

The one man to survive survived
because as a boy he'd died for three minutes
and didn't like what he'd seen.

When we met on the Plains of Abraham
he asked if I'd ever visited his grave.

The Chambermaid

In the spring of 1914 the west wind
blew a clump of human hair
into the Archduke Ferdinand's hunting-lodge.

The Archduke was twelve kilometres away
hunting deer with an elderly Junker.

While the other servants discussed
the uses of phrenology in Viennese society
the mute chambermaid swept up the hair
and brought it to her room —
where she arranged it to resemble
a map of her native Serbia.

And that was the last anyone saw of her.

Fairytale Doctors

They shine a pencil-light in my left eye
and tell a joke about 'I' and 'You'.

They throw salt in my face.
A grain lodges in my third eye
and I glimpse Ptolemy's Adri deserta
sinking under the weight of one hundred and fourteen
   dragonflies.

They breathe fire on me.

They lay eggs on my charred tongue.

Mexico

It is 1866 and the Emperor Maximilian,
his equerry, and twelve hussars,
rest in the shade of some alamos.
A diamondback rattlesnake slithers by
without their bothering it.

One week later the revolutionary leader,
Benito Pablo Juarez,
will shoot the rattlesnake,
skin it, and have it for supper.

In a year's time Juarez will be president
and the emperor will have been executed
by a firing-squad.

Only the rattlesnake knows all this.

Two Plus One

There was one survivor of the disaster.
His lifeboat had drifted for a week
before our yacht came into sight.
He said his name was something
out of the Old Testament.
I called him Abraham.

When he began to run a temperature
my wife interrupted her study
of Kremer and Ptolemaic cartography
to steer a course for the nearest port —
that being in the Marshall Islands.

Sixty miles from our destination
there was a flash on the horizon.
The rest is H-bomb history.

My wife and Abraham became lovers.
She died of bowel cancer
the year I swam the Hellespont.
Abraham died of leukemia
the year I desecrated my wife's grave.
I succumbed to a variety of cancers
the moment I realised two plus one
added up to whatever I pleased.

Twig

The wolf tore the throats out of five sheep.
Three brothers trailed it for three days,
until they lost it on Deehommed Mountain.

Suddenly afraid they turned for home.
Close to journey's end they made camp
on the edge of a forest as yet unnamed.

As they slept the wolf came out of the forest,
and transformed itself into a sharpened twig
at the heart of their dying fire.

Stare

As he woke from a dream of the moment of death
she said she had come to agree with him
concerning their dispute over the date
on which the civil war had ended —
the day their maternal grandfathers were executed
within a stone's throw of one another.

As he washed off the traces of the night
she stared at the two hairline cracks
in the porcelain jug he held in his hands,
and wondered where and when they would meet.

Black Friday

The black cloud appeared at 8 a.m.
Grandmothers told their grandchildren
to stay indoors until it passed
or else they would be kidnapped
by a man in a black suit
and murdered in a basement
stinking of rat-piss and dog-shit.

Here and there across town
this warning went unheeded.
By dusk the remains of seven children
had been found floating in the canal.

The victim's grandmothers
met on Saturday morning
to express their satisfaction
that there was still one day in the year
when they could not be ignored.

Last Respects

The door creaks open into a moonless midnight
And a courtyard filled with open coffins:
After zigzagging among the corpses
You walk back into a big house
Reeking of the Bessarabian perfume
Worn by the priest and the wolf.

You paid your last respects to a family
Who barely tolerated your presence —
Who told Anne to do better for herself,
As you went from darkened room to room
In the hope of finding her alone.

You are slumped in an armchair.
Your mouth is sour. You have just dreamt
Her father's final dream.

Nagasaki

I arrive in the city
to sell the skull
of Saint Thomas Aquinas
to a retired policeman.

A passer-by tells me to panic.

I prise open the nearest door,
climb to the third floor,
and walk in on a geisha
listening to herself on the radio
describe how she navigated by the stars
out of her dead mother's womb.

She asks why she sweats blood
when I touch her where I shouldn't.

I wake up clinging onto
the second horseman of the Apocalypse
in his disguise as the tail-fin
of a high-altitude American bomber.

New Star

They carried her body on a door
across a bog and through a cromlech
to be buried in a pit of lime
by an astronomer and a lens-grinder.

And after her wails died away
the door was pitched onto a bonfire
lit to celebrate the naming of a new star
after the star which was there before.

Sukkoth: The Ninth Day

The Orange Free State: a shebang
a hundred Irish miles north of Bloemfontein.

And, yes, it goes without saying
they promised not to come back for us.

◈

We stepped into the shadow of the fire
they'd kindled the night we were born.

It is true they discovered our remains
and buried us where we'd buried them.

Shadows

In Manchuria the conjugal bed was placed
in the darkest corner of the room,
where the seed was stored, and above
the spot where the dead were buried.

You told me this as we saved
an acre of your dying husband's hay.
Remember how I wouldn't look you in the eye
when I asked how long he'd been given?

You said it couldn't happen soon enough,
and left me standing there, certain
I'd never know what to make of you.

In my mind's eye I saw a fresh grave
crisscrossed with the shadows
we'd become of ourselves.

The Chill Wind

Because the chill wind ordered me
I opened the triple-locked door
To the malnourished Talitha.

And then the wind insisted
I take her to a restaurant
Whose gazpacho makes insomniacs
Of everyone who clears his bowl.

Through the night of December 21st
We debated Bachelard's opinion
That cold is a symbol for solitude.

Next morning she slept through the thaw
I had negotiated with the wind,
After promising it a door in my house
To bang open and shut forever.

Elijah's Wagon

On a day in September
which was like an Ash Wednesday —
gun-metal sky, nuns and priests everywhere —
I climbed onto Elijah's wagon.

We travelled no more than a mile —
from Stoker's Lodge
to the grave of the supposed vampire
Countess Elisabeth Bathory.

At the going down of the sun
Elijah left me there alone
to meditate on her epitaph:
'Fearful yet to be feared.'

By the time he returned
the Countess was at my feet.
She said her epitaph should have read,
'Here lies an emigrant of light.'

Elijah threw her in the back of the wagon
and set it on fire.
Though the wagon screamed,
she did not.

The Arrow

In the New Era's seventh year the Chief of the Yellow Flags set out on a bamboo horse from his father's burial-place to his mother's burial-place — a distance of some seven hundred koals.

On this journey he had to travel through the Territory of Forking Paths. It was while crossing this land that a pebble lodged in one of the horses's hooves and crippled it. He threw the pebble over the horizon, set the horse on fire, and crawled to his destination like a beaten slave.

There were seven of us hanging in the air when he reached the burial-ground. But the number seven meant nothing to him — not even when I went through his seven shirts and seven skins to pierce his seventh soul.

The Church

After being locked for thirty years
the church door was so rusty
it couldn't be opened —
not even by my right shoulder
and my left foot.

Finally I took an axe to it.

Inside I discovered
two hundred cobwebs and one spider,
the egg-shaped soul of my grandmother,
and a dark corner
in which I could lay down to sleep
knowing I'd wake up.

Awe

I woke up in a vessel icebound at the pole.
Two sailors were standing guard over a pile of nails
as their delirious captain searched for a candle
to light their way home.

When the captain jumped ship
and disappeared into a blizzard
the two sailors swallowed the nails
and asked me to do something equally bizarre:
I took command.

Right up to the moment of their deaths
they seemed to stand in awe of me.

Talk of the Devil

In eleven of the town's twelve districts
the talk was that she had given the devil —
in the shape of a wolf —
the run of her house.

The mayor said he would swear to this
on the graves of his mother
and his mother's mother.

She told me this as we sat
on the steps of the Black Church,
watching my fellow militiamen
drill in the square.

Much to her amusement
I said she would soon find herself
looking down the barrel of a rifle —
and into the eyes of a wolf
in my clothing.

The Jackdaw

The jackdaw perches on a butcher's shop-sign,
eavesdropping on two old women
lamenting the fact they're losing
fragments of their memory.

One of them wants to know
the name of the street
police headquarters used to be on.
The other one shrugs her shoulders
and says she was raped by a policeman
on the morning of her fifteenth birthday.

The jackdaw loses interest in them
when they begin to discuss
the possibility that the street,
rather than police headquarters,
has been moved.

The jackdaw flies the half-kilometre
to the Jewish Cemetery.
A man who had been a concert-pianist
is being buried this afternoon.

When the man's wife begins to cry
the jackdaw flies fifty kilometres
to play 'Three Blind Mice'
on a baby-grand which has been out of tune
since August 1968.

At dusk the jackdaw collides
with a truck that is not a truck,
which is carrying allegories and metaphors
the powers that be declared
as having stood the test of time.

The Royal Asylum

The wind blows a newspaper into the gardens
at the rear of the Royal Asylum's A-wing.
The Empress Dowager picks it up
and reads that her son has declared war
on a country she has never heard of —
there's a huge photograph of him
sitting in the shade of an oddly familiar tree.

She buries the paper in the compost heap
and turns her attention back
to the felling of the oak
five successive emperors hanged themselves from.
Her son is perched high in that tree,
waiting for it to give him the order
to surrender unconditionally.

Death of a Fabulist

It is predicted by my grandmother
that the general will spend his final hours
chasing a basilisk through a mosque,
performing his wife's mastectomy,
imploring his mistress to smell of the pampas,
and dotting the I's of his *roman à clef* —
the story of a compulsive fabulist,
torturer, wife-beater, cheat.

As the general is able to fly,
walk on water, and make himself invisible,
it will be difficult for his assassins
to know if they have been successful.

When they think they've shot him
they'll hide in a field of barley
and listen to their hearts thump
and wonder if they can be sure
he didn't soar into the air,
stroll across the River O —
or disappear in front of their eyes.

Their worst fears will seem to come true
when the general appears among them.
But they'll have no cause for alarm
unless they are afraid of a ghost
with a story to tell.

Treachery

Her last note to him said, 'What we remember of treachery is how we said it, and how we should have said it'. A few hours after she posted it she was dead — ambushed by the police at the junction of May the 14th Street and June the 23rd.

When it came to pass that he couldn't bear to keep the note out of his sight, he telephoned the police and accused himself of betraying the motherland. The recorded voice he spoke to was his own.

Eve

She ate a rotten apple for breakfast.
At lunch she coughed up blood.
During dinner she cleaved the plate in two.
After supper she read the despised Gombrowicz.

        ✣

A bare flat reeking of garlic, venison,
and a blocked-up toilet. My gums are bleeding.
Because I've made her in my own image
she refuses to stick the needle in her neck.

        ✣

We'll kiss with our eyes sewn shut.
She'll roll onto her empty stomach.
I'll produce a viper from behind her left ear.
She'll insist we not despair of one another.

Fontaine the Stoat and Valentine the Hare

In the back room of the Comrades' Tryst
Fontaine and Valentine were drinking schnapps
and demanding absolute fidelity of one another.

As I approached their table
they smiled indulgently
at the sight of my clenched left fist.

Five chairs were thrown in the air,
two tables were smashed against the wall,
and the earth's axis tilted by one degree

before we came to agree
that the townland of Derryvarymore
was home to more than a stoat and a hare.

The Left Hand of Oblivion

Because my mother was forty-three
when she conceived me
I was born left-handed.

Lying in the cradle
I examined my left hand
and decided to lose it on a day
when the sky was especially blue and grey.

Seven years later I lost the hand
to a red and yellow threshing machine —
the same day my mother's plane
flew into Lookout Mountain.

It was my mother
who informed me of her death,
as I lay in the back of a hearse
travelling toward oblivion —
wherever and whenever that may be.

Savage

This is the story a blind man told me as we waited in Astor Place for a downtown train that never came.

'Because he was on the losing side of a brutal civil war, Pedro Savage fled to the United States and hid for ten years in the basement of the house his grandmother Escobar bought on New York's Sixth Avenue, to celebrate (let us suppose) the assassination of her first cousin and second husband — one General Rodrigo O'Donnell.

'It is a fiction that when Savage left the basement he stared straight at the noonday sun and did not blink his eyes. The truth is Savage kept his eyes shut until dusk, when seven invisible and nameless beasts surrounded him for the final kill on every avenue of the Americas.'

The Tiger's Tail

I insist that anyone
who steps on the tiger's tail
and lives to tell the tale
yawns when asked if he was afraid
and swallows his tongue
when told he must do it again.

Why are you wiping the cold sweat from my forehead
as I tell you this?

Mother, don't worry if the answer
is so far beyond you
there is a cramp in your stomach,
a lump on your breast,
and a meteorite hurtling toward
the back of your right hand.

In Time of Plague

My aim was true and the arrow
hit the boar above its left eye;
but when I got down on my knees
to give thanks to the Lord
it came back to life and charged.
I stretched my bow but then put it aside
as the boar swerved around me
and made for a servant girl
fleeing the plague to the south.

That evening, in a cold room
in the house of my uncle Frederik Bachofen,
the girl served me the boar for supper
and spread the plague to yet another.

Three Days of the Cho War

On the eleventh day of the war
I administered Jethart justice
to three rebels
and then got unconscious with drink.

On the twelfth day
I cleaved a rabid dog in two
with nothing more
than a switch of hazel.

The twenty-second day was the day
I set a match to a mandrake root,
an acre of *Saccharum Officinarum*,
and three-quarters of my own sweet self.

On the Block

That humid August afternoon
she squatted at the foot of my bed
and cut the buttons off
my white shirts and black jackets,
as I told her how my childhood was spent
singing songs to a sycamore tree
about the manifold uses of axes.

Nothing was more certain than
that when I finally nodded off
it would be with my head at rest
on the freshly scrubbed chopping-block
she'd bought in part exchange
for a silver thimble, a golden thread,
a heart of heart's needle.

Closing the Book

Once I travelled for a day and a night
To open the book outside a prison
And pray for a killer and his executioner.

When I caught a whiff of burning flesh
I blanched and drove off in a Chevrolet
A dust-devil had turned from red to grey.

Near a place called New Calvary
I turned a corner on two wheels
And crashed into a Joshua tree.

In a dream I followed that tree east —
Where, because the dark was afraid of me,
It was already first light.

God was so angry with me
For dreaming without his permission
That he ended the world

By skipping the last chapter,
And closing the book on me
With an almighty bang.